THE
PRAYER
OF
PROTECTION
STUDY GUIDE

D0324509

ALSO BY JOSEPH PRINCE

Reign in Life

The Prayer of Protection

The Power of Right Believing

100 Days of Right Believing

Grace Revolution

Grace Revolution Study Guide

Glorious Grace

Destined To Reign

Unmerited Favor

100 Days of Favor

Healing Promises

Provision Promises

Health And Wholeness Through The Holy Communion

A Life Worth Living

The Benjamin Generation

Your Miracle Is In Your Mouth

Right Place Right Time

Spiritual Warfare

For more information on these books and other inspiring resources,
visit JosephPrince.com.

JOSEPH PRINCE

THE
PRAYER
OF
PROTECTION

STUDY GUIDE

LIVING FEARLESSLY IN DANGEROUS TIMES

Faith
Words

New York • Boston • Nashville

FaithWords
Hachette Book Group
1290 Avenue of the Americas
New York, NY 10104
faithwords.com
twitter.com/faithwords

First Edition: November 2016

FaithWords is a division of Hachette Book Group, Inc.
The FaithWords name and logo are trademarks of Hachette Book Group, Inc.

The publisher is not responsible for websites (or their content) that are not owned by the publisher.

The Hachette Speakers Bureau provides a wide range of authors for speaking events. To find out more, go to www.hachettespeakersbureau.com or call (866) 376-6591.

Literary development: Lance Wubbels Literary Services, Bloomington, Minnesota.

ISBN: 978-1-47894-470-6

Printed in the United States of America

10 9 8 7 6 5 4 3 2 1

CONTENTS

꧂

INTRODUCTION

$\sim\!\!\mathcal{N}\!\!\sim$

We live in dangerous times. A time in which a person could be attacked by terrorists while watching a concert. A time during which an epidemic from one country could spread to another through a single traveler. A time when earthquakes, floods, and other calamities seem to be happening all too often. A time of violence, conflict, and wars.

In the midst of all this, there is good news—a message of hope—for you and your loved ones. Good news of the promises in God's Word that will fortify you and equip you during these times. Good news of His protection and favor upon you. The Scriptures tell us that as darkness covers the earth, "the LORD will arise over you, and His glory will be seen upon you" (Isa. 60:2).

This tells us that while the darkness and dangers in this world are certainly real, God's promise that you can live protected and untouched can be an even greater reality in your life.

Why is this so important for you to know? Because our loving Father in heaven doesn't want you, His beloved child, tormented by fear. Fear of terrorism and wars. Fear of losing your job or of an illness leaving you with no future. Fear for your children and their safety. God's Word tells us, "There is no fear in love; but perfect love casts out fear" (1 John 4:18). When you encounter and experience the Lord's perfect love for you, *every* trace of fear is expelled from your heart.

Whatever fear it is that grips your heart today, I believe that as you use this study guide to meditatively go over God's protection promises for you in *The Prayer of Protection*, you will be anchored in His love for you, and learn faith-building truths that will strengthen you. You'll learn how you can pray the prayer of protection found in Psalm 91 and walk in divine protection, as well as divine wisdom to stay safe. I know you'll also be deeply encouraged as you study the amazing testimonies from people around the world who have experienced God's protection firsthand.

Beloved, there are so many beautiful pictures of the Lord's awesome protection in His Word that will garrison your heart with faith and hope. It is my prayer that as you journey through these powerful revelations contained in *The Prayer of Protection* via this study guide, you will be empowered to truly live confidently and fearlessly in these dangerous times!

HOW TO USE THIS STUDY GUIDE

❧

I'm delighted that you've chosen to use this study guide that was written as a companion to my book, *The Prayer of Protection: Living Fearlessly in Dangerous Times*. This study guide will show you how you can pray the prayer of protection found in Psalm 91, as well as uncover what the Bible says about divine protection and learn powerful truths that I know will strengthen you.

This study guide has been created so that it lends itself to both self-study or personal development, as well as small-group study or discussion, say in a care group or book club setting. Whichever the purpose you have in mind, you'll find ample opportunity to personally encounter the Lord as you take time to study and meditate on His Word, and hear His Spirit speak and minister His grace to your heart and mind.

The format of each chapter is simple and user-friendly. To get the most out of each chapter, it would be best to first read the corresponding chapter in the parent book, *The Prayer of Protection*. That'll give you more background and understanding. If you're not sure how to answer a certain question that is based on a teaching in the parent book, there's a helpful answer guide at the back you can refer to. It covers all the questions except for those that require a personal response from you.

If you decide to use this study guide in a small-group setting, a good habit is to do some preparation before each meeting. Take some time to read the relevant portions of text and to reflect on the questions and how they apply to you. This will give your group study depth and make the sessions much more fruitful and productive for all.

Because of the personal nature of this study guide, if you use it in a group setting, remember to keep any sensitive or personal content that is shared within the group! Confidentiality, courtesy, and mutual respect lay the foundation for a healthy, safe group. Commit yourself to listening in love to your fellow participants, encouraging one another in the revelation of the Scriptures and of the truths that you are discovering together, and show each participant patience and grace.

Beloved, whether in personal study or with a group, I am believing with you that each session will be most inspiring. May you find yourself walking increasingly in the Lord's protection and living confidently and fearlessly in His love for you!

Psalm 91

He who dwells in the secret place of the Most High
Shall abide under the shadow of the Almighty.
I will say of the LORD, "*He is* my refuge and my fortress;
My God, in Him I will trust."

Surely He shall deliver you from the snare of the fowler
And from the perilous pestilence.
He shall cover you with His feathers,
And under His wings you shall take refuge;
His truth *shall be your* shield and buckler.
You shall not be afraid of the terror by night,
Nor of the arrow *that* flies by day,
Nor of the pestilence *that* walks in darkness,
Nor of the destruction *that* lays waste at noonday.

A thousand may fall at your side,
And ten thousand at your right hand;
But it shall not come near you.
Only with your eyes shall you look,
And see the reward of the wicked.

Because you have made the LORD, *who is* my refuge,
Even the Most High, your dwelling place,
No evil shall befall you,

Nor shall any plague come near your dwelling;
For He shall give His angels charge over you,
To keep you in all your ways.
In *their* hands they shall bear you up,
Lest you dash your foot against a stone.
You shall tread upon the lion and the cobra,
The young lion and the serpent you shall trample underfoot.

"Because he has set his love upon Me, therefore I will deliver him;
I will set him on high, because he has known My name.
He shall call upon Me, and I will answer him;
I *will be* with him in trouble;
I will deliver him and honor him.
With long life I will satisfy him,
And show him My salvation."

1

THE SECRET PLACE

He who dwells in the secret place of the Most High
Shall abide under the shadow of the Almighty.
—Psalm 91:1

❧❧

Despite the fact that there is a lot of fearmongering everywhere we turn today, it is vital that we do not let fear take over our hearts. As believers, we have no business feeding on fear. If your mind is entangled with knots of anxiety, it's time to start living by what the Lord Jesus has purchased for you at Calvary.

To help you do this, let me share with you a powerful key from the very first verse of Psalm 91, the prayer of protection. The Hebrew word for "dwell" is *yashab*, which means to *sit down*, to remain, or to settle. So the very first thing that God wants you to do to enjoy His protection is to rest. His protection, peace, love, and other blessings flow in your life when you are in a place of rest.

1. The Bible says that we are *seated with Christ* at God's right hand (see Eph. 2:6, Heb. 1:3). What does the word "seated" mean, and what has Christ done that allows us to dwell in the secret place of the Most High?

Now, because of the completed work of our Lord Jesus, we can have free access into the presence of our *Elyon*, the Most High. We can abide under the shadow of the Almighty or *Shaddai*.

2. How do these two Hebrew names of God—*Elyon* and *Shaddai*—in the first verse of Psalm 91 alone help to put our problems in perspective?

3. How do you feel, knowing that our Lord Jesus through His finished work has paid for God's divine protection over every area of your life? Spend some time giving thanks to the Lord and share with Him how this blesses you.

Read Carina's amazing testimony of healing. In it, she mentioned that God took little Caylen into the "secret place" where he was safe and received healing.

4. Is the "secret place" a place that only an elite few can go to?

5. Where is the "secret place" and how do we get there? How do you feel, knowing the answer?

6. When the flood came, the ark protected and saved Noah and his family. What two powerful lessons can we take away from the ark, which is a type of Christ, our salvation?

The more you grow in your revelation and valuation of what it means to be in Christ—being in the secret place of inseparable closeness with Him, where you have His loving presence constantly with you, watching over you, and protecting you—the more you'll find your heart at rest instead of filled with worry and fears.

7. What can you do to continue growing in your valuation of being in Christ and what will happen as you do?

8. What does being under the shadow of the Almighty speak of?

9. What message of divine protection is found in the testimony of the businessman who was miraculously shielded from the bomb that exploded right outside the hotel lobby where he was?

10. If you hold on to God's Word for deliverance when you are faced
    with problems, how does the enemy respond? What choices are
    you then presented with?

The Lord has put a *now* word in my heart for the times we are living in, and that word is "protection." He also told me that there are
people reading this who might think, *I have claimed the promises of
Psalm 91 before and it didn't work.* If you have the same thought, I want
to encourage you to hold on to His Word. Whatever your experience
has been, the Word of God stands eternal and unshakable. If you have
not experienced full protection in the past, I believe that as you hold on
to His Word and persevere in faith, you will walk more and more in the
Lord's total protection.

11. What does Job 5:19 and John 16:33 tell us about "troubles," and
    how can we strengthen our hearts with regard to them?

Deliverance from trouble is fantastic, but there is a promise that is even greater, and that is when you are at that place where "no evil shall touch you" (Job 5:19). That's my prayer for you and your loved ones. While we live in dangerous times, we have an almighty God who watches over us. May we all increase and have a progressive revelation of the Lord's protection in these last days.

12. After reading this chapter, what did you discover about the prayer and promise of divine protection? Write a prayer to the Lord, telling Him how you feel as you reflect on these truths.

2

"I WILL SAY"

I will say of the LORD, "He is my refuge and my fortress;
My God, in Him I will trust."
—Psalm 91:2

⌘

Wwhat are you saying of the Lord today? Are you saying He gave you the trouble you are presently in to teach you humility? Are you saying, "Sometimes the Lord heals, and sometimes He gives diseases"?

If you are saying these things about the Lord, then it's time to change what you believe about Him. If you really believe that God is the author of your problems, would you really be running to Him for help?

1. The psalmist declared that the Lord was his "refuge" and "fortress." What do these words mean and what are you declaring when you say them?

Perhaps you have not been saying *anything* about the Lord at all. Perhaps God seems far away and you feel cut off from Him. If that is you, take a break today from whatever you have on your busy to-do list and simply take time to dwell in His sweet presence. See yourself in His secret place. Abide under His shadow. Savor His favor. Receive His wisdom. And find rest for your troubled soul.

2. What has God promised you in Hebrews 13:5 about His presence? What did our Lord Jesus accomplish so you can always have God's presence, and take Him as your refuge and fortress?

Say to yourself, "The Lord is with me and I have His favor, blessings, and protection." Sense His shadow covering you. His shadow is a picture of nearness. You are not trying to get into the secret place; you are *already* there in Christ. In Christ, you can't get any closer to God.

3. The picture of the father running toward the prodigal son best captures the heart of God. How does knowing this comfort you when you feel as if God is a million miles away?

To trust in God doesn't mean that there will be no butterflies in your stomach. Trust means that even though you have the butterflies, you still act on God's Word. Whatever it is you are afraid of doing, do it afraid while keeping your trust in the Lord.

Each of the names of God has a divine attribute, and understanding and believing that He is each attribute will cause that attribute to flow into our lives and bring comfort and strength when we feel afraid. Always know that while there are benefits to studying the names of God, the most powerful name is the name of Jesus.

4. How do the two names of God in the first verse of Psalm 91 strengthen us when we feel afraid or weak?

5. In the second verse of Psalm 91, God is referred to as *Yehovah* or *Yahweh*. What does that name mean and how does that relate to Jesus' name in Hebrew, *Yeshua*?

6. Read Jennifer's powerful praise report. Explain what it means to *actively listen* based on what you have learned from Hebrews 4:2.

Believing begins on the inside. Faith begins on the inside. When the Word of God is preached, faith is the hand that takes. Faith says, "That's mine! The promises of God's protection are *mine!*" What begins inside is then reinforced outside—you begin to speak the Word out loud, and begin to see His promises manifest in your circumstances.

7. Write down and begin to commit to memory three Scriptures about faith and speaking that will help you understand and walk in greater faith.

Faith involves *believing* in your heart as well as *speaking* with your mouth. You and I are made in God's image. When God first saw darkness, He called forth light by speaking. He *said*, "Let there be light" (Gen. 1:3). In the New Testament, our Lord Jesus *spoke* to the storm and it subsided. He *spoke* to the demons and they fled. He *spoke* to the sick and they were healed. He *spoke* to the dead and they lived.

8. When we are faced with darkness in any area of our lives, what should we be doing?

9. What powerful principle is reflected in Brenda's praise report that will help you to build a shield of faith around your heart?

I encourage you today to build a shield of faith around you and your family. *Listen* to Christ-centered messages, *believe* the Word of God, and *speak* out loud the promises you want to see manifesting in your life. I believe that the Lord wants to seal this truth in your life today.

10. Do you desire to experience a shield of protection around you and your family? Write or print out the confession at the end of chapter 2, place it where you will see it every day, and declare it every morning. Alternatively, you can also write out your own confession of faith.

3

RIGHT PLACE, RIGHT TIME

Surely He shall deliver you from the snare of the fowler
And from the perilous pestilence.
—*Psalm 91:3*

◈

Surely He *shall* deliver you from the snare of the fowler. Not "maybe" or "sometimes," but an unqualified "surely." Not a conditional "He *might*," but a definitive "He *shall*." What blessed assurance we have that our God *will* deliver us from the snare of the fowler!

The Bible depicts the devil as a fowler. A fowler is a professional bird catcher. He lays traps and carefully conceals them so that he can ambush unsuspecting birds. The Bible also depicts the devil as a thief and murderer who comes to steal, kill, and destroy (see John 10:10).

1. What do we need to understand about the world we live in, and what can we rejoice in despite the snares of the fowler?

2. In the natural, we will see the world getting darker and darker. There is a very real and active fowler who is setting up snares. As believers, explain why we do not need to live in fear.

3. What does King Solomon tell us about "winners" in Ecclesiastes 9:11?

4. Solomon then goes on to talk about those who are "like fish taken in a cruel net" or "birds caught in a snare" in verse 12. What two categories of people is he depicting when we compare verses 11 and 12?

We want to be among the group of people to whom "time and chance happen." The Hebrew word for "time" is the word *eth*, meaning time or season. The Hebrew words for "chance happen" are *pega qarah*. Together with *eth*, they present a picture not of random occurrences, but "right happenings" that are dependent on *the Lord's orchestration*.

5. The root of the word *pega* in the Scriptures is from the word *paga*. What does *paga* mean and how is it first used in Genesis 23:8?

6. The other Hebrew word, *qarah*, is often used in other parts of the Bible to explain God-ordained happenings. So what does "chance happen" (*pega qarah*) more accurately refer to, and when you have *eth* and *pega qarah* combined here, what does it speak of?

7. The first mention of *eth* ("right timing") in the Bible appears in Genesis 8:11 within the phrase "in the evening." What connection do you see between right timing and "the dove"?

8. The dove bore an olive leaf in its mouth. What message does this tell us about how the Holy Spirit leads and protects us on a practical basis?

9. *Eth* appears in the phrase "in the evening" not only in Genesis 8:11, but in other parts of the Bible as well (see Gen. 24:11, Josh. 10:27). What is the connection between the evening time and the time of our Lord Jesus' finished work at the cross? How does this revelation enable you to live fearlessly?

The first time *qarah* is mentioned is in Genesis 24:12, where it is translated into the phrase "please give me success." The servant of Abraham asked God to give him *qarah*—right happening. Doesn't that remind you of what we said earlier about *pega qarah* being "prayed happenings"?

10. **What does the posture of the servant teach us about the importance of prayer?**

I want to show you one last thing about the phrase "but time and chance happen to them all" (Eccl. 9:11). Look at the phrase as written in Hebrew:

The two highlighted Hebrew characters—*Aleph* and *Tav* (reading from right to left)—are the first and last letters of the Hebrew alphabet. They are usually left untranslated in the Hebrew.

11. **Who do the letters *Aleph Tav* point to and how does that apply to you?**

12. What does the praise report of the lady who was protected from a terror attack in a hotel and Sandy's report of divine protection when stuck in traffic tell us about being Jesus-conscious in our daily lives?

The prayer of protection is not an incantation. It is not some magical chant that grants you protection. It is all about intimacy and relationship with the Lord. Prayer is a conversation. There is no relationship if there is no conversation. So talk to Him, commune with Him, involve Him, and listen to Him. He will lead and guide you to be at the right place at the right time with the right people.

13. Write a prayer to the Lord, telling Him how you feel as you reflect on what you have learned in this chapter, and thank Him for His protection and intervention in the past, present, and future.

4

CONSENT TO COME UNDER HIS WINGS

He shall cover you with His feathers,
And under His wings you shall take refuge;
His truth shall be your shield and buckler.
—Psalm 91:4

❦

Let's never take for granted how wonderful it is that we are safe in the secret place of *El Elyon*, the Most High God. We are under the shadow of *El Shaddai*, the Almighty God. *Yahweh*, our Lord, is our refuge and fortress. *Elohim*, the Creator of the heavens and earth, is our God and in Him we can trust! But you know what? There's so much more to God's divine protection. Let's look now at Psalm 91:4.

1. To understand the words "His wings" and "feathers" in verse 4, we can look at the ark of the covenant, focusing on the cherubim on top. Describe the ark and explain why it was the most holy furniture piece in the temple and how it typifies our Lord Jesus Christ.

To understand the significance of the mercy seat, we have to understand the contents within the ark of the covenant.

2. Three items were placed inside the ark of the covenant. What were they and what did they represent?

3. God took these three items, placed them in the ark of the covenant, and covered them with the mercy seat. How is the mercy seat a picture of the secret place of divine protection that God wants us to live in every day?

In Old Testament times, on Yom Kippur, or the Day of Atonement, after the high priest went into the Holy of Holies and sprinkled the blood of an innocent animal on the mercy seat, all God saw of the ark of the covenant was the blood, and no longer the rebellion and failure of man.

4. What happened on Yom Kippur was only a *shadow* of what was to come through our Lord Jesus. Explain why.

5. Read Exodus 25:17–22 carefully. Where does the Lord promise to meet us and to speak to us? What message is He speaking to us today?

6. In John 20:11–12, what did Mary see as she looked into the tomb? What assurance does the empty tomb provide?

Veronica's praise report reminds us that there is no safer place in the universe than under God's wings, which is pictured beautifully in a mother hen protecting her chicks.

7. Read Jesus' lament and subsequent weeping over Jerusalem in Luke 13:34–35 and Luke 19:43–44. Describe the Lord's tender mercies toward Israel.

8. The Lord will not force on us His protection if we are not willing to come under His wings. Are you willing to take Him as your refuge? Write a prayer telling Him your response.

The Lord does not want you to simply claim His promises of protection. He wants you to come close to Him. Running to Him and coming under His feathers speak of closeness. It's not about how many times you have recited Psalm 91; it's about having an intimate relationship with Him. And the reason we can have intimacy with God and come boldly to His throne of grace today lies in what He did for us at the cross.

9. How was Jesus, the perfect offering, greater than the fires of judgment?

10. What does Victoria's praise report of being spared from carbon monoxide poisoning vividly illustrate for us?

11. Psalm 91:4 ends with this proclamation: "His truth *shall be your* shield and buckler." What do the words "shield" and "buckler" tell you about God's protection?

12. What are you learning about taking refuge under God's wings? Take a moment to give thanks to the Lord and share with Him how this blesses you.

5

FEARLESS LIVING

You shall not be afraid of the terror by night,
Nor of the arrow that flies by day,
Nor of the pestilence that walks in darkness,
Nor of the destruction that lays waste at noonday.
—*Psalm 91:5–6*

I love how Psalm 91 reminds us that we have round-the-clock protection. Whether it is at night or in the day. Whether it is in darkness or at noonday. Whether we are faced with a terror or confronted by arrows. Whether pestilences threaten or destruction looms. We do *not* have to be afraid because our God, who watches over us, neither slumbers nor sleeps (see Ps. 121:3–4).

The reality is, the world we live in seems to be engulfed in negative news, and fear seems to be the most normal response. But I want you to know that in the midst of all that is happening in the world, you *can* be fearless, and this comes from knowing the Lord as the God of peace.

1. **What is the result when God manifests Himself as "the God of peace" in your life?**

If you are living solely by your obedience and merits, the devil has power over you because he can always point to something that you have not done. If you claim God's protection and healing based on what you have done, the devil will point to one thing you have failed in, and all your faith implodes. You will disqualify yourself mentally and inwardly from receiving whatever you might be trusting the Lord for.

2. Grace is the only thing against which the devil has no defense. Explain why this is true.

First John 4:18–19 says that when you have a revelation of God's perfect love for you, every fear in your life will be cast out. To the extent that you understand His love, you will live fearlessly in dangerous times.

3. How does a growing understanding of God's grace give you a greater revelation of God's perfect love for you?

"Jehovah Shalom" is Hebrew for "the God of peace." Hence, when Paul (being Jewish) said "the God of peace be with you," he was saying "*Jehovah Shalom* be with you."

The first appearance of the name *Jehovah Shalom* in the Old Testament is found in Judges 6. We read here that the Midianites were terrorizing Israel day and night, and Gideon was bound by fear and overcome by the never-ending news of terror that surrounded him.

4. Who appeared to Gideon in the midst of his fear, and what did this person call Gideon (see Judg. 6:12)?

5. When we feel besieged by fear and want to hide from all the dangers around us, how does our Lord Jesus see us? What assurance and hope does this give us?

When God becomes *Jehovah Shalom*, the God of peace, in your life, He doesn't just soothe your emotions. He will *lead you with His peace.*

6. How can you experience the Lord leading you with His peace when you are making an important decision?

7. Gideon's response to the Lord's calling him a man of valor was to complain and express his anger at God. What was the Lord's astounding reply to Gideon and what encouragement does this give us (see Judg. 6:14)?

When Gideon realized he had been speaking to the Angel of the Lord and began to panic, the Lord said to him, "Peace be with you; do not fear, you shall not die" (Judg. 6:23). So Gideon built an altar there to the Lord and called it "The-LORD-Is-Peace" (Judg. 6:24), or in Hebrew, *Jehovah Shalom*. This is the first time the name *Jehovah Shalom* appears in the Bible.

8. What does the word *shalom* mean?

When Psalm 91 says you shall not be afraid of "the pestilence that walks in darkness," it speaks of every epidemic, every virus, every deadly disease, and every outbreak. When it mentions "the destruction that lays waste at noonday," it covers all accidents and outward destruction. When it talks about the "arrow that flies by day," it covers all projectiles, including even modern missiles that can shoot down planes.

9. When you face one of the above threats, such as an unknown disease developing in your body, how can you respond without fear?

When you take God as your *Jehovah Shalom*, this is what He says to you: "Do not fear, you shall not die."

During the outbreak of severe acute respiratory syndrome (SARS), a heavy cloud of fear hung over my nation of Singapore. I preached by faith on *Jehovah Shalom*, and by God's amazing grace *not one person* who was attending our church regularly died from this deadly virus.

10. Read Tracy's praise report of how the Lord delivered her brother from a life-threatening disease after she pronounced God's protection and provision over him. While *in the natural* there are many legitimate reasons for us to be fearful, why can we be free of fear?

11. Write out John 14:27 and as you meditate on it, allow the Lord Jesus to be your refuge and receive His supernatural peace that will guard your heart and mind.

May *Jehovah Shalom* fill your heart and set you free to live fearlessly in these dangerous times!

6

IT SHALL NOT
COME NEAR YOU

A thousand may fall at your side,
And ten thousand at your right hand;
But it shall not come near you.
Only with your eyes shall you look,
And see the reward of the wicked.
                                    —*Psalm 91:7–8*

As believers, we are in a spiritual war, and we should not be ignorant of the enemy's tactics. How does he attack us? By assaulting us daily from all directions with tragic newsflashes, doctors' reports, and other negative information. The projectiles he shoots may not come with arrowheads or be filled with gunpowder, but they are no less deadly. His weapons come in the form of crippling thoughts and crushing fears. We need to learn how to combat these oppressive thoughts.

1. When negative thoughts come your way, how do you usually respond? How can you keep them from taking root?

We can't stop the enemy from attacking our minds, but we can surely defend ourselves with the sword of the Spirit, which is the Word of God (see Eph. 6:17). God's Word is infallible, unshakable, and everlasting (see Isa. 40:8, 1 Pet. 1:25).

2. Read Matthew 4:1–11. How did our Lord Jesus respond to the devil's attacks? What does this tell us about the way we overcome the devil's temptations?

3. Some people are afraid they will die young of the same disease their parents died of. How can they use the written Word to overcome this fear? Take a moment to reflect on how knowing you can use the written Word of God against this (or any other) fear helps you.

If you have been entertaining crippling, fearful thoughts, NOW is the time to rise up and make this declaration: "A thousand may fall at my side and ten thousand at my right hand, but it shall NOT come near me!" (see Ps. 91:7).

4. For something to happen *at your right hand* means that it has to be really close to you. Are you afraid of something that is happening really close to you? Use the written Word of God to overcome that fear now and write it down.

5. It is not enough for you to merely *know* the Word in your heart. Why do you also need to *say* it?

Fear is not something you can reason or analyze away. Fear is irrational. And it doesn't go away by itself. The only way to defeat fear is to speak the Word of God to whatever fear you have by saying, "It is written."

6. Write out 2 Timothy 1:7. Take some time to memorize this powerful verse of Scripture. Now, speak this verse out loud. Do you feel the power that comes with saying it aloud?

7. What should you do when a fear that you've declared the Word against comes back?

8. Search out and write down the Scriptures that cover the areas of your worries and needs, and arm yourself with God's written Word!

9. Megan's awesome testimony illustrates the power of the written Word released in our situations through our mouths. What Scripture did Megan take hold of and why did she choose it?

10. Read the incredible testimony of the Jewish believer who served as a paratrooper in the Israel Defense Forces during the fourth Arab-Israeli war in 1973. What Scripture strengthened him to never fear being hit by bullets and how did it get into his spirit?

I encourage you to believe that through the Lord's divine protection over you, your life will reveal the same faithfulness and power of God to others!

The devil is known as "the accuser of our brethren" (Rev. 12:10). He will always try to keep you self-occupied and in fear. God wants you Christ-occupied and in faith! When the devil tries to plant fears in your heart, take up your shield of faith and declare, "It is written." Whatever the danger, it shall not come near you!

11. Based on what you have learned in this chapter, take a moment to reflect on how you can start living every day with full assurance of faith and confidence in God's protection promises.

Memorize Psalm 91 and when you are under attack, quote it the way our Lord Jesus quoted Scripture. Meditate on Psalm 91 and allow yourself to be fortified by this prayer of protection. There is such a power and authority that comes with quoting the pure and unadulterated written Word of God. Start walking in that power and authority today!

7

DWELL SAFELY IN CHRIST, YOUR REFUGE

Because you have made the LORD, *who is* my refuge,
Even *the Most High, your dwelling place,*
No evil shall befall you,
Nor shall any plague come near your dwelling.
—Psalm 91:9–10

⚬⚭

Many years ago, I was meditating on these very verses from the prayer of protection when a power drill I was operating somehow slipped out of my hands and went straight toward my stomach. Although the power drill was spinning at full force, when it hit me, it just miraculously bounced off!

The Word of God does not say that no evil shall befall "the world." It says that "no evil shall befall **you**, nor shall any plague come near your **dwelling**," which includes your family (boldface mine). Let this Scripture strengthen and anchor your heart. Because you have made the Lord your refuge, protection from strains of viruses that science does not yet have a cure for—Ebola, Zika, or AIDS—is God's promise to you and your family!

1. Psalm 118:8 says, "*It is* better to trust in the LORD than to put confidence in man." How does the Hebrew word for "trust" relate to taking the Lord as your refuge and what does that tell us?

Back in the days when the children of Israel entered the land of Canaan, if someone unintentionally killed a person, the closest relative of the deceased had the legal right to avenge him. In His mercy, the Lord appointed six cities of refuge for people who had committed unintentional manslaughter (see Josh. 20:3, Deut. 19: 4–5 NLT).

2. The cities of refuge are a beautiful picture of our Lord Jesus. In His mercy, what did our Lord Jesus do for us at the cross?

3. Does the devil still have a legal right to put a death sentence over the head of a believer because of his sins today? Explain why not.

The fact that there are no insignificant details in the Bible is seen when we uncover the hidden truths concealed in the names of the six cities of refuge. Read Joshua 20:7–8, then carefully read through and consider the meaning of the names of the cities in order of their appearance.

4. When we put the six names together, what message and what stunning picture of Himself does the Lord provide us? Whatever you may be going through right now, how does this strengthen you?

5. In the parable of the lost sheep, when the shepherd found the lost sheep, lifted it up, and laid it upon his strong shoulders, the sheep did nothing but consent to be rescued. Correspondingly, what does God invite us to do today?

The Bible tells us that the shepherd lays the sheep on his shoulders "rejoicing" (Luke 15:5). Our Lord rescues us with great joy in His heart and a big smile on His face.

6. How does Deuteronomy 33:12 describe Jesus as the safest place of refuge that you, His beloved, can be in?

There is another type hidden in the teaching on the cities of refuge. The six cities are scattered across the land so a person can flee to the nearest one to take refuge. It is a picture of local churches scattered all around the world.

7. What makes the local church a place of refuge?

8. Our Lord is above every principality and power and every name. In our fallen and broken world today, where can the fullness of His power be found?

9. Read the praise report from the couple in Dallas whose marriage was saved by being in a church and having the wise counsel of leaders who walked the journey with them. What message from their story do you feel God is speaking to your heart about the importance of being planted in a local church?

Psalm 92:13 tells us that "Those who are planted in the house of the LORD shall flourish in the courts of our God." Beloved, if you are not regularly attending a local church, I want to encourage you to be planted in one. As you do so, may you, your career, your marriage, and your household flourish in every way!

The King James Version of Psalm 91:9–10 says you can make the Lord your *habitation*. First John 4:16 says, "God is love, and he who abides in love abides in God, and God in him." The more you stay in His love, the more God Himself becomes your dwelling place. No evil shall befall you and no plague shall come near your dwelling.

10. Psalm 46:1 says, "God *is* our refuge and strength, a very present help in trouble." How was God a "very present help" when a cyclone hit the area where Iris lived? What did Iris declare?

11. Read the powerful declaration at the end of chapter 7 and use it to boldly look to the Lord and be completely at rest.

8
ACTIVATING HIS ANGELS

For He shall give His angels charge over you,
To keep you in all your ways.
In their *hands they shall bear you up,*
Lest you dash your foot against a stone.
—Psalm 91:11–12

❧

As you read the exciting story of the prophet Elisha and the king of Syria, put yourself in the shoes of Elisha's servant who woke up and found the entire city he was in surrounded by enemies intent on killing his master and him.

1. Surrounded by the enemies' troops, horses, and chariots, what seemingly illogical words did Elisha speak to his servant (see 2 Kings 6:16)? Take some time to meditate on this powerful Scripture and commit it to memory.

2. Then Elisha prayed a simple prayer that the Lord would open his servant's eyes. What did the servant see when his eyes were opened?

3. Why was the young servant fearful while Elisha was fearless?

4. If you are in a constant fight with fear, what Scriptures can you fortify your heart with (see 2 Kings 6:16 and Isa. 54:17)? How can you start to apply this in your battle against a specific fear today?

5. According to Psalm 91:10–11, the way the Lord keeps us from all evil and all plagues is by deploying His angelic army. What does God giving His angels "charge" over us mean? What assurance of protection does this give you?

Psalm 91:11–12 was misquoted by the devil when he brought our Lord to the pinnacle of the temple and said to Him, "If You are the Son of God, throw Yourself down. For it is written: 'He shall give His angels charge over you,' and, 'In *their* hands they shall bear you up, lest you dash your foot against a stone.'" To this Jesus replied, "It is written again, 'You shall not tempt the LORD your God'" (Matt 4:5–7).

6. Why did the devil leave out the words "to keep you in all your ways" after saying, "For He shall give His angels charge over you"?

7. Psalm 91:11–12 has nothing to do with endangering yourself to test God's protection (in contrast to the way Satan used it). What powerful truth does it tell you about how God watches over you in your daily walk?

8. Jesus said if believers drink anything deadly, it will not hurt them (see Mark 16:18). How does this apply to your life?

9. Psalm 103:20 also tells us that angels "do His word." According to the NLT and Amplified versions, what does Psalm 91:11–12 say about the Lord's instructions to His angels?

The Word of God tells us that when the archangel Lucifer fell, one-third of the angels fell with him. Do you know what that means? It means that two-thirds of the angels are still on God's (and our) side.

10. When Jesus was arrested, He said that more than twelve legions of angels, or 80,000 angels, were at His disposal. Why did He not pray and activate those angels to deliver Him?

11. What is one way you can activate angels in your life?

12. When you worship our Lord Jesus, His angels camp all around you, surrounding you to deliver you. Take some time to express your heart in worship to Him, thanking Him for His goodness and His angels that surround you like a protective shield.

Another important key that activates God's angels is speaking or declaring the Word of God. Psalm 103:20 tells us that angels heed "the **voice** of His word" (boldface mine).

13. **How do you give voice to God's Word?**

Sophia's praise report described how a vintage car pulled in front of her car and shielded her and her daughter from the flying debris of an exploded tire. Another testimony from a key pastor in our church told of how he and his wife were spared being exposed to a highly contagious virus at a hotel that they had tried and tried but were unable to secure a room.

14. **Take some time to go back over this chapter and meditate on how legions of angels are poised to minister for you personally, and see God's heart for you. What are you discovering about God's protection that you, like Elisha's servant, may not have realized before your eyes were opened?**

9

TIME TO PLAY OFFENSE

You shall tread upon the lion and the cobra,
The young lion and the serpent you shall trample underfoot.
—Psalm 91:13

✕

There is no question that the world is a fallen place and that the devil is the god of this world (see 2 Cor. 4:4 NASB). The apostle Peter tells us, "Be sober, be vigilant; because your adversary the devil walks about **like a roaring lion**, seeking whom he may devour" (1 Pet. 5:8, boldface mine). But get this truth into your heart today—we, as believers, are not called to cower in fear like the people of the world. The devil may be the ruler of this fallen world, but God's eternal Word proclaims that "He who is in you is greater than he who is in the world" (1 John 4:4).

1. What authority do we who are in Christ have, according to Psalm 91:13?

2. How was that authority demonstrated when Samson was suddenly ambushed by a lion?

3. What spiritual truth does the honey represent for us today?

The prayer of protection in Psalm 91 has many defensive elements—
dwelling in the secret place of the Most High, abiding under the shadow
of the Almighty, taking the Lord as our refuge and fortress, being covered under His wings, and being protected by an angelic army. But
the prayer of protection does not end there. Psalm 91:13 declares our
offensive position where we take authority and go on the attack.

Jesus said, "Behold, I give you the authority to trample on serpents
and scorpions, and over all the power of the enemy, and nothing shall
by any means hurt you" (Luke 10:19). That is the power and authority
we have as believers today! The devil has no dominion and power over
you. He is a defeated foe. His proper place is not to rule over you, but to
be *beneath your feet* (see Gen. 3:15, Eph. 1:22).

4. In the praise report from Gisele, how did she and her husband
   exercise their authority when they heard the doctor's report?
   Is there a similar situation you are facing that you can apply
   this to?

5. The sword of the Spirit, which is the Word of God, is the only
   piece of the armor of God that is offensive (see Eph. 6:14–17).
   When we pray the prayer of protection in Psalm 91, what are
   we doing?

6. Why does the devil go about "like a roaring lion, seeking whom he may devour" (1 Pet. 5:8) and not some other creature? Are you familiar with the sound of his roar?

7. Why does Satan want you to have the impression that God is mad at you, that you have failed Him and are under His condemnation?

8. How does God see you and what confident assurance does this give you against the "roaring lion"?

9. Proverbs 19:12 says, "The king's wrath *is* like the roaring of a lion, but his favor *is* like dew on the grass." What happened to God's wrath against our sins and what place has His favor brought us to today?

Read Sally's testimony and be encouraged by the power of the prayer of protection when it is based on our revelation of our righteousness in Christ.

I am not saying that there's no suffering in the body of Christ. None of these protection truths shared from God's Word negates the fact that we are called and given the privilege to suffer persecution for His name's sake (see Phil. 1:29–30, 2 Tim. 3:12 NLT, and Matt. 10:22).

10. What does this persecution involve and also not involve?

11. Job was a righteous man who experienced terrible suffering. Why is what happened to Job not something that will happen to you who are IN CHRIST today? What do we have that Job did not?

12. Because our Lord Jesus became our ransom, what did His perfect sacrifice at the cross accomplish for you?

13. Carefully read Philippians 1:21–25, Acts 14:19–21, Acts 28:3–6, and 2 Timothy 4:6–8. How do these Scriptures speak of the apostle Paul as a man who had power over life and death?

14. How does Psalm 91:16 correct the erroneous teaching that says "when your time comes" you will die and have no say in the matter? Take a moment to thank the Lord for the freedom that knowing this brings.

10

PROTECTED BY THE FATHER'S LOVE

"Because he has set his love upon Me, therefore I will deliver him;
I will set him on high, because he has known My name."
—*Psalm 91:14*

Growing up, I have heard many teachings that make it seem like you have to *qualify* for God's blessings. They make it sound like God blesses you *only* if you are able to love the Lord with all your heart, with all your soul, and with all your mind. They conclude that God's protection is dependent on us fulfilling the condition of loving the Lord perfectly.

Such teaching robs you of the faith to believe God for divine protection over yourself and your loved ones, because no one is able to fulfill this requirement of loving God perfectly.

1. Even when our love for God fails, what qualifies us for God's protection? What is the crux of the new covenant of grace and how does it put peace in your heart?

We are under the new covenant of God's amazing grace, where we can depend on *His* unconditional, unchanging, and irrevocable love for us!

Under the old covenant, God's protection *was* conditional. But we are no longer living under the old covenant. We have a new and living way (see Heb. 10:20)! Under the old, protection is *achieved*. Under the new, protection is *received*. At the cross, God "made Him who knew no sin *to be* sin for us, that we might become the righteousness of God in Him" (2 Cor. 5:21). Today, we *are* the righteousness of God in Christ!

2. Because we are righteous in Christ, what promise can we receive with regard to God's protection (see Ps. 5:12)?

3. Psalm 91:14 says, "Because he has set his love upon Me, therefore I will deliver him." How do we set our love upon God?

4. Daniel in the Old Testament set his mind and heart on the Lord's love for him. Read his story carefully in Daniel chapter 6. What elements from Psalm 91 do you see in this account of God's protection and deliverance?

5. Daniel had a habit of praying three times every day, giving thanks to the Lord. Is this a formula to walking in divine protection? What can we learn from this with regard to developing an intimate relationship with the Lord?

6. For you who are in Christ, why can't the devil come to the King and demand that you be punished?

7. Based on King Darius's suffering over sending Daniel into the lions' den, what torment must our Father in heaven have gone through to send His own beloved Son to the cross?

Psalm 91:14 says, "I will set him on high, because he has known **My name**" (boldface mine). We have talked about seeing four names of God in just the first two verses of Psalm 91 alone, and how that brings revelation and comfort to us.

8. Our Lord Jesus came to reveal only one name. What is it and what difference does it make to know this name?

9. In John 17:11, when Jesus prays for our protection, He uses the word "keep." What does the word in Greek mean, and who keeps and guards us?

The glorious testimony of healing and resting in the Father's love from a professional athlete who attends our church in Dallas speaks of the power in knowing that the all-powerful, almighty God of Israel is not someone far away. He paid the price so that you and I can *draw near* to Him.

10. Joseph in the book of Genesis wanted his family to dwell in Goshen. What does Goshen mean and why did he want them living there? How does that apply to us today?

11. What two things were special about the land of Goshen during all of the ten plagues that besieged the land of Egypt?

12. We live in days where we see a supernatural darkness cover the earth. Yet, what do the Scriptures tell us that we can experience?

Beloved, God makes a difference between His people and the people of the world. We are His. He desires for us to be close to Him so that He can hide us under the shadow of His wings. He paid the price so that we can be called His children. Oh, what manner of love the Father has given unto us, that we should be called the sons and daughters of the Most High (see 1 John 3:1)!

13. God is your Father. Your Daddy. Your Abba. Take a moment to say or write a prayer to Him, thanking Him that He is drawing you into an intimate relationship with Him. Tell Him how it feels to be under His protection.

Whatever may be happening in the world, you can be bold and fearless because the Word of God proclaims, "Neither death nor life, nor angels nor principalities nor powers, nor things present nor things to come, nor height nor depth, nor any other created thing, shall be able to separate us from the love of God which is in Christ Jesus our Lord" (Rom. 8:38–39)!

11
WISDOM TO STAY SAFE

"He shall call upon Me, and I will answer him;
I will be with him in trouble;
I will deliver him and honor him."
—*Psalm 91:15*

❧

We have a God who wants us to run to Him. And the moment we do, He has promised that He *will* answer us. Not "might," or "perhaps," but a definite "will." And He does not stop at merely assuring us that He will answer us. He goes on record for all eternity, saying, "I **will** *be* with him in trouble; I **will** deliver him and honor him" (boldface mine).

1. When we call upon the Lord, why can we have the assurance that He will answer us?

2. Whenever we are troubled and anxious, what are we to do?

Read the powerful promise of Psalm 46:1–3. We do not need to fear because even in times of turmoil and trouble, He is our very present help, our refuge, and our strength! Our part is to call upon Him and He will answer and deliver us.

3. Melinda and her son were miraculously spared from all harm in the car accident. What was the one thing that she did?

4. When Shadrach, Meshach, and Abednego refused to bow before the king's statue, what unflinching statement of faith did they make about God's protection (see Dan. 3:16–18 NLT)?

5. How did God honor the three young men's faith? What is the only thing the roaring flames did to them?

Beloved, the God of Shadrach, Meshach, and Abednego is *your* God!

There is truly no other god who can rescue like our God. Whatever circumstances you might be thrown into, our Lord Jesus is the fourth man with you *in the midst* of the fire. Deuteronomy 31:6 says, "Be strong and of good courage, do not fear nor be afraid of them; for the LORD your God, He *is* the One who **goes with you**. He will not leave you nor forsake you" (boldface mine). He is with you in the midst of your adversity. When Jesus is with you, nothing can harm you!

6. The fire had absolutely no power over the three friends. It did not even leave a trace of smoke on them! What assurance does that give you when you face a trial?

7. Meditate on this beautiful picture of God's divine protection that keeps you untouched by the very dangers that surround you. How do you now see your life and your future knowing this?

There's such assurance knowing that the Lord can deliver us from trouble. But better than being delivered from trouble is not getting into it in the first place. I've found that often, we can stay protected and out of trouble when we follow the Holy Spirit and lean on His wisdom when making decisions. Every day, we need His wisdom, just as we need His protection. Proverbs 4:7 tells us that "wisdom *is* the principal thing," and in all our getting, we need to *get wisdom.*

8. What does 1 Corinthians 1:30 tell us about wisdom? How can we avoid many troubles and dangerous situations?

Proverbs 11:14 tells us that we need to apply wisdom and heed the Lord's leading through the wise counsel of the people around us, such as our leaders in the local church and our spouses.

9. If godly counsel spoken over our lives can help us not to make foolish decisions, reflect on how you tend to respond to the wisdom and counsel you receive from your leaders in your local church, and how you can better gain from it.

10. What principle can we learn from Isaiah 11:2–3 that will help us to make wise decisions rather than unwise decisions?

The more areas of your life you involve the Lord in, the more you can experience His protection. The apostle Paul even allowed the Holy Spirit to guide him in something as seemingly natural as his travel itinerary. He obeyed when the Spirit forbade him to preach in Asia and Bithynia (see Acts 16:6–7).

11. **What does this tell us about closed doors?**

12. **Does being led by the Spirit have to be something complicated?**

Let's take up the Lord's invitation to involve Him as we go about our lives every day. Call upon Him today and He will answer and lead you.

Apart from the four names of God that we covered in the first two verses of Psalm 91, there is a fifth name of God that is concealed in the very last word of Psalm 91—"show him My **salvation**" (boldface mine).

7. **What is the Hebrew word for "salvation" and how is it related to our having long life?**

8. **Jesus came and showed us His salvation by sacrificing Himself on the cross for our sins. How long of a life did He purchase for us? How secure does that make you feel about your salvation in Him?**

Some people teach that when you sin, you lose your salvation and have to get born again all over again. The enemy uses this erroneous teaching to incessantly attack some believers with thoughts of a lost salvation.

9. **What verse in 2 Timothy answers this with the truth of the Lord's protection and preservation unto eternity? Meditate on it often and confess it boldly if these oppressive thoughts ever attack you.**

The Bible often speaks of "the fear of the Lord." I believe in a reverential honor of the Lord. But I am not for any kind of teaching that promotes the idea that God wants you to be afraid of Him. God welcomes us to dwell in His secret place, to be so close to Him that we come under His shadow. Hebrews 4:16 says, "Let us therefore come boldly to the throne of grace, that we may obtain mercy and find grace to help in time of need." These are all pictures of intimacy. In any relationship, fear and intimacy cannot coexist. If you fear God today, you won't be able to believe Him for His protection. That is why it is so important for you to be strong and established in His grace.

10. How did Jesus define the fear of the Lord and why is it so important to accurately understand the fear of the Lord?

11. The testimony of how the Lord guided and protected the lady from Virginia and her daughters while they were on a road trip bears out how practical the Lord is in looking after all our needs and keeping us safe. What message from their story do you feel God is speaking to your heart?

Amos 9:11 contains a prophecy that speaks of our time: "On that day I will raise up the tabernacle of David, which has fallen down, and repair its damages; I will raise up its ruins, and rebuild it as in the days of old."

12. What interesting feature about the tabernacle of David is in contrast to the tabernacle of Moses?

13. At the precise moment when our Lord Jesus died on the cross, "the veil of the temple was torn in two from top to bottom" (Matt. 27:51). What is God saying to us?

On the night of the first Passover, when the children of Israel applied the blood of an innocent lamb on their doorposts, God said to them, "Now the blood shall be a sign for you on the houses where you *are*. And when I see the blood, I will pass over you; and the plague shall not be on you to destroy *you* when I strike the land of Egypt" (Exod. 12:13). Jesus became that innocent lamb that was sacrificed for us when He shed His blood and died on the cross.

14. None of us can ever do enough to merit God's protection, but praise be to God, as believers we are qualified by the blood of Jesus Christ! Take a moment to come to your loving Savior and pray the prayer of protection, Psalm 91. Then write a simple prayer of worship and thanks for His protection over you and your entire household.

Today, as believers in Christ, His blood protects us. May our confidence be in His blood and not in our own merits to earn God's protection. Let us come boldly to worship our Lord in the tabernacle of David where there is no veil. Come boldly under His wings and worship the Lord daily with the prayer of protection and receive His protection for you and your entire household!

CLOSING WORDS

Throughout this study guide, I've endeavored to share with you what the Lord has revealed to me down through the years about the prayer of protection found in Psalm 91. It has been a tremendous privilege for me to talk to you about the promises of protection that we can stand upon as beloved children of the Most High. I pray that His Word has anchored your heart in faith and cast out every fear as you took this journey with me.

While it's true that we live in dangerous times, we have our Abba's promise that we can live safe, secure, and protected no matter what turmoil may be around us. Our heavenly Father does not want His children partaking of the fear that has invaded the hearts of people of the world. In fact, He wants *every* trace of fear expelled from your heart, knowing that He has set you apart and that He who watches over you *never* slumbers nor sleeps! When fear comes knocking, let God's promises of protection fill your heart, mind, and mouth, and the God of peace, our *Jehovah Shalom*, will come into and move in your situation!

Our Lord Jesus desires to have an intimate relationship with us and He loves it when we acknowledge our need for Him. He loves it when we allow Him to hide us under the shadow of His wings, close to His heart of love. The prayer of protection is not some magical chant or incantation that grants us protection. Our protection in the Lord is all about us being intimate with and close to Him. As you involve Him in your day-to-day life, you will see Him lead you by His wisdom and protect you from making unwise decisions. And I pray that you will see His protection manifest more and more as you grow in your revelation of how deeply loved you are by the Lord, who protects like no other.

ANSWERS

✂

CHAPTER 1

1. The word "seated" means that you are no longer depending on your self-efforts. Under the old covenant, the priest had to offer the morning sacrifice at 9 a.m., and then remain standing for six hours until after the evening sacrifice at 3 p.m. Our Lord Jesus was crucified at 9 a.m. and He hung on the cross for six hours until He died at 3 p.m., thus fulfilling the type of both the morning and evening sacrifices (see Heb. 10:11–12). Because Jesus became the final sacrifice, the work of the priest is done and he no longer has to stand. Because our Lord cried, "It is finished!" at Calvary (John 19:30), we are today *seated* in Christ (see Eph. 2:6). We can dwell in the secret place of the Most High—a place of peace, safety, and security—because the blood of our Lord Jesus has paid for every blessing of protection in Psalm 91!

2. In and of ourselves, our present challenges may appear insurmountable. But when we are resting in the presence of *El Elyon*—God Most High, the possessor of heaven and earth (see Gen. 14:19)—and abiding under the shadow of *El Shaddai*—God Almighty, the all-sufficient One—all of a sudden, our adversities don't seem so intimidating after all.

4. No, the Lord's blessings are not just for an elite few who somehow qualify. If a blessing is from our Lord, *everyone* can have access to it. The young and the old, the strong and the weak, the rich and the poor—*all* have access by faith to His blessings that are freely given.

5. The secret place of the Most High is a place where you are *in Christ*. How did you get to be in Christ? By receiving the Lord Jesus as your personal Lord and Savior. Once you are a born-again believer, our heavenly Father sees you in Christ. You are safe, protected, and secure in *the* hiding place!

6. First, the ark didn't have windows along its sides, only near the roof. The truth here is that God does not want you to focus on all the darkness, terror, and evil that are around you and in the world. He wants you to look up and know that His Son is coming back for you.

Second, whenever Noah lost his balance and fell as the storm waters crashed against the ark, he fell *in* the ark; he never fell *out* of the ark. Similarly, for the believer today, when the devil tempts you and you fall, you don't fall out of your position in Christ, you are still *in* Christ. In the book of Proverbs, it says, "For a righteous man may fall seven times and rise again" (Prov. 24:16). You see, a believer doesn't fall in and out of righteousness. Our righteousness today is a gift from our Lord Jesus Christ (see Rom. 5:17). This means that even though we may fail from time to time because we are imperfect human beings, we are still in Christ our ark and do not forfeit His blessings of protection.

7. Keep hearing anointed preaching that reveals who you are and what you have in Christ. Study the Word of God and keep hearing grace-based teachings on God's promises to protect you, as well as praise reports of God's grace and protection over His people. As you do, you'll begin to value being in the secret place more and more. You'll wake up every morning confident of His tender care, protection, and preservation. You'll live life full of hope and zest instead of worry and fear, and see Him deliver and protect you from whatever the enemy may throw at you.

8. Being under the shadow of the Almighty speaks of closeness, intimacy, and protection. It speaks of a place of refreshing, coolness, and rest. When Psalm 91 talks about dwelling in the "secret place" of the Most High, that secret place is not a geographical location, but *spiritual intimacy* with our Lord Jesus.

9. Our Lord Jesus watches over His own! If this man had not reached the pillar at the precise moment the bomb went off, he would have been directly in the destructive path of the explosion. Only our Lord Jesus can put us at the right place at the right time and keep us in His divine protection.

10. The enemy is so afraid that the Word will become firmly rooted in your heart that he will come immediately to try to steal the Word from your heart. He will point to your outward circumstances and taunt you with thoughts such as, "Look, your child is still sick—where is God now? Where is the reality of Psalm 91?" You can either back away from God's Word and agree with the enemy, or you can stand in faith and continue to believe His promises. My prayer is that you will continue to stand on His Word.

11. These Scriptures tell us that in this world, we will have trouble. The fact that God declares in His Word that He will deliver us from troubles tells us we will experience troubles. But God wants us to know that the more we hear preaching on Psalm 91, the more we quote it and remind ourselves of His protection daily, the more our faith in His protection will grow (see Rom. 10:17).

CHAPTER 2

1. The Hebrew word for "refuge," *machaceh*, refers to a shelter from storms and danger. This shelter is like the bunkers that many Jews have in their homes in Israel today to shelter them from small-scale attacks. In the figurative sense, when you say the Lord is your *machaceh*, you are also declaring that He is your place of hope.

In Hebrew, the word used for "fortress" is *matsuwd*. It refers to a castle or stronghold, a place of defense and protection against large-scale attacks. Whatever you might be going through right now, you can declare that the Lord is your refuge and your fortress—your protection in both small as well as big attacks. *He* is your shelter from all danger *and* your place of hope!

2. He has promised in His Word that He will never leave you nor forsake you (see Heb. 13:5). Our Lord Jesus paid for you to have access to God's constant presence. At the cross, He cried out, "My God, My God, why have You forsaken Me?" when God turned His back on Him (Matt. 27:46). He took our place and was rejected by God when He carried our sins so that today, we can take His place of being in the constant presence of the Father and take Him as our refuge and fortress.

3. The picture of the new covenant is God sending His only Son, Jesus Christ. It is the picture of the father running toward the prodigal son in spite of his failures. Under the new covenant, we are seated with our heavenly Father in Christ and we see the smile on His face! That is how close you are to God today. So even if your feelings tell you that God is a million miles away, learn to trust His Word over your feelings. All you need to do is to utter the words "Father" or "*Abba*," and immediately you will sense that He is closer than your own breath.

4. The first name of God mentioned in Psalm 91 is "Most High" (*Elyon*), which means He is the Most High God and there is no one higher than Him. He is the possessor of heaven and earth (see Gen. 14:19). The verse goes on to refer to God as the "Almighty." In Hebrew, it is *Shaddai*—the God who blesses you with more than enough, more than you can contain. Man has limitations but we have a God who is abundantly unlimited.

5. *Yehovah* or *Yahweh* means the covenant-keeping God. Jesus' name in Hebrew, *Yeshua*, actually means "*Yahweh* saves." It is not "*Yahweh* judges." The name *Jesus* means "*Yahweh* SAVES." If you are broke, *Yahweh* saves. If you are sick, *Yahweh* saves. If you have enemies that are coming against you, *Yahweh* saves. Whatever saving you need, Jesus is the answer, for His name means "*Yahweh* saves."

6. The author of the book of Hebrews describes what it means to listen actively: "For indeed the gospel was preached to us as well as to them; but the word which they heard did not profit them, not being mixed with faith in those who heard *it*" (Heb. 4:2). I pray that as you "listen" to the words in this book, you are coming alive and mixing your faith with the promises of Psalm 91. Many people heard me preach on the prayer of protection, but you can tell that Jennifer ran with the teaching, mixing it with her faith to the point that she began to share the psalm with her family members and declare the power of God's protection over them.

7. Romans 10:9 tells us that "if you **confess** with your **mouth** the Lord Jesus and **believe** in your heart that God has raised Him from the dead, you will be saved" (boldface mine). Our Lord Jesus also said, "Whoever **says** to this mountain, 'Be removed and be cast into the sea,' and does not doubt in his heart, but **believes** that those things he **says** will be done, he will have whatever he **says**" (Mark 11:23, boldface mine). And the apostle Paul wrote, "since we have the same spirit of faith, according to what is written, 'I **believed** and therefore I **spoke**,' we also **believe** and therefore **speak**" (2 Cor. 4:13, boldface mine).

8. We should be calling forth what we want to see! If we find ourselves caught in a dangerous situation, we should declare, "The Lord is my refuge and my fortress." If there is a sickness in our body, we can call forth our healing by saying, "Thank You, Jesus, by Your stripes I am healed!" Start speaking forth your protection, your health, and your victory today!

9. The principle reflected is the importance of investing your time in getting God's living and powerful Word into your heart. Brenda was filling herself up with the promises of God's protection. When the Lord gave her a vision of her son being in danger, her heart was already full of faith (not fear) and she *spoke* out with authority against the evil coming against her son. When she heard about her son's accident, she was listening to preaching on Psalm 91. She was already building a shield of faith around her heart. Faith comes by hearing and hearing the word of Christ (see Rom. 10:17 NASB).

CHAPTER 3

1. We need to understand that the world we live in is a fallen world. Adam committed high treason and gave his authority over this world to the devil. Because of what Adam did, the devil is the ruler of this world. The apostle Paul calls him "the prince of the power of the air" (Eph. 2:2). That is why as long as the devil is still the ruler of this world, the world will continue to get darker and darker and there will continue to be accidents, sicknesses, calamities, tragedies, and deaths.

But we can rejoice in the knowledge that the devil's lease on this world is quickly running out. Apostle Paul also tells us that our Lord Jesus is coming back and all His enemies will be humbled or put under His feet, with death as the last enemy to be destroyed (see 1 Cor. 15:26).

2. Our trust is in our Lord Jesus. We are *in* this world, but we are not *of* this world (see John 17:16). We have a Savior who is even more real than this world, and He has promised to deliver us from the snare of the fowler and from perilous pestilences (dangerous diseases and viruses). The bottom-line is, we need to realize how much we need our Savior and His protection daily. We need to involve the Lord Jesus in our lives every day. Only *He* can deliver us and keep us safe!

3. King Solomon tells us that the winner of the race is not necessarily always the fastest one, and the person who wins the battle isn't necessarily always the strongest. He points out that men of understanding are not the only ones who gain riches, and men of skill do not always experience favor. And then he says this: "Time and chance happen to them all."

4. There are two categories of people—those who are blessed because they find themselves at the right place at the right time, and those who are caught off guard in an evil time and find themselves at the wrong place at the wrong time.

5. *Paga* means to make intercession or pray. In Genesis 23:8 (NIV), it means "intercede." The same word is also used in Isaiah 53:12 where it says the Lord "**made intercession** for the transgressors" (boldface mine).

6. "Chance happen" should more accurately be translated as "prayed opportunities" or "prayed happenings." When you have *eth* and *pega qarah* combined here, it speaks of right-time, right-place happenings, or of being at the right place at the right time, doing the right thing as a result of prayer.

7. The first mention of right timing has to do with the dove—a picture of the Holy Spirit. It's the Holy Spirit who can guide you to be at the right place at the right time.

8. The olive leaf was a message of peace to men. It tells us that the message the Holy Spirit brings is one of peace. The Holy Spirit leads us on the wavelength of peace. Sometimes, when you are about to do something, perhaps sign an agreement, plan a vacation, or take part in some activity, you might feel a lack of peace. If that happens, please stop and take time to pray about what you are about to do, because the Holy Spirit speaks to us through the peace (or lack of it) He puts in us. He doesn't speak to us through nagging or accusations. He leads us through peace. When there is no peace in your heart, it's time for you to reevaluate your decision and listen to His leading, for your protection.

9. The Old Testament priests had two daily sacrifices, one in the morning at 9 a.m. and the other in the evening at 3 p.m. Jesus was crucified at 9 a.m. and He died at 3 p.m., thus fulfilling the type of both the morning and evening sacrifices. At the time of the evening sacrifice, all the judgment had fallen on the body of Jesus. The floods of God's judgment were ended by the sacrifice of Christ. The Holy Spirit comes to you speaking peace, telling you that there is now no enmity between you and God, because judgment has passed. Today, you can live without fearing God's judgment.

10. He prayed for God's help, intervention, and leading. To pray is to adopt a posture of humility (the proud don't pray). It is saying to God, "Father, I can't, but You can." No matter how intelligent we are, we can't put ourselves at the right place and right time a hundred percent of the time. Only the Lord can do this for us. If we humble ourselves to hear Him, He will guide us and protect us. The Bible says, "The humble He guides in justice, and the humble He teaches His way" (Ps. 25:9).

Psalm 91 is the *prayer of protection*, because when we pray this prayer, we are saying, "Lord Jesus, we can't protect ourselves, but You can. We humble ourselves before You. Be our refuge, our fortress, and our God. Surely You shall protect us and deliver us from harm in these dangerous times. Lead us to be at the right place at the right time and to be with the right people."

11. Our Lord Jesus said, "I am the Alpha and the Omega" (Rev. 1:8, 11). The New Testament is written in Greek, but Jesus being a Jew must have said, "I am the *Aleph* and the *Tav*." He is the first letter and the last letter. The beginning and the end. So the letters *AlephTav* point to our Lord Jesus, who has the first and final word on your situation. Your diseases don't have the last word, He does. Your problems don't have the final say, He does.

Jesus' signature is inscribed in Ecclesiastes 9:11. This means that our Lord Jesus is the One who brings the *eth* and *qarah* together in your life! When your heart is full of and dependent on our Lord Jesus, you'll end up at the right place at the right time supernaturally!

12. Don't take your protection for granted. Even with something as mundane as driving on the road or going to breakfast, pray for the Lord's protection. Your trust is in the Lord's protection. Include Jesus in your schedule. Allow the Holy Spirit to lead you. When you are truly led by the Lord, it will lead to good success and victory.

CHAPTER 4

1. Of all the furniture pieces in the temple, the ark was the most holy. It was placed in the Holy of Holies, and typifies our Lord Jesus Christ. It was made of incorruptible wood and overlaid with gold. The wood represents His incorruptible and sinless humanity, while the gold speaks of His perfect divinity and deity. Our Lord Jesus was one hundred percent man and yet one hundred percent God. The lid of the ark of the covenant, where you find the cherubim, is hammered out of one solid piece of gold. It is called *kapporeth* in Hebrew and is usually translated as "mercy seat."

2. The three items placed inside the ark of the covenant were the stone tablets on which God had inscribed the Ten Commandments, a golden pot of manna, and Aaron's rod that had budded. The three items typify man's rebellion—man's rejection of God's holy standards, man's rejection of God's provision, and man's rejection of God's appointed leadership.

3. It is a beautiful picture of His unmerited favor over our lives, of how mercy triumphs over judgment. This is the secret place where God wants you and me to live each day—not under the claws of judgment, punishment, and condemnation, but under His wings of mercy, grace, and favor. This is the place of divine protection.

4. Under the old covenant, the blood of the animal sacrifices only *covered* the sins of the children of Israel for one year. What happened on Yom Kippur was only a *shadow*. Our Lord Jesus is the *substance*. He is the Lamb of God who *takes away* the sins of the world, and His sacrifice on the cross was once and for all (see John 1:29, Heb. 9:12)! Once Jesus' blood has cleansed us of our sins, God does not see us in our sins anymore.

5. He will meet us and speak to us "from above the mercy seat." God's message to us is about His mercy and grace, about Jesus' shed blood, and about His finished work. There are people who are preaching from the judgment seat, preaching about the law and how we have fallen short. The wages of sin is death. Under the law, there is no escaping death. But God's message for today is all about His mercy, grace, favor, love, and protection. Under grace, Jesus died our death on the cross. He was punished with the death we deserved for our sins. He gave up His protection on the cross, so that we may walk in divine protection today. Hallelujah!

6. Mary saw the *substance* of the ark of the covenant. Just as there were two cherubim or angels on the mercy seat, there were two angels sitting where Jesus had lain—one at the head and the other at the feet. The tomb is empty because our Savior paid the full price for our sins with His own blood and He is risen! Our hope, confidence, and assurance of salvation are found in the nail-pierced hands of our resurrected Savior. The mercy seat is a picture of the throne of grace (see Heb. 4:16). That is where we want to be—at the throne of grace, under the protective covering of His feathers and His wings.

7. The Greek word for "wept" in Luke 19:41 is *klaio*, and it means to be so affected emotionally as to sob and wail aloud. The Lord's tender mercies toward Israel were so strong that He shed much tears over her. He wished that He could gather Israel under His feathers as a mother hen gathers her chicks under her wings, but Israel rejected Him. The Lord could not force His protection on them because they were not willing to accept it.

9. When Jesus was offered on the cross, He absorbed the judgment of God in His own body, and, as the offering, He was greater than the fires of judgment because He was not consumed. On that cross, our Lord declared, "It is finished!" *before* He gave up His Spirit. The Offering remained *after* all of God's judgment was exhausted. Hallelujah!

10. It vividly illustrates how the Lord protects us whenever we simply come boldly to His throne of grace and humbly consent to come under His wings. We should take every opportunity to do this.

11. A buckler refers to a small round shield used for close-contact fighting. A shield is much larger, one you can dig into the ground and hide behind when spears, arrows, or rocks are being launched at you in a bigger attack. So whether it is a small or big attack, His truth—your shield and buckler—covers you completely!

CHAPTER 5

1. Romans 16:20 tells us this: "And the God of peace will crush Satan under your feet shortly. The grace of our Lord Jesus Christ *be* with you. Amen." He will crush every fear, every worry, and every anxiety!

2. Grace is the undeserved, unearned, and unmerited favor of God. That is why we put our faith in the blood of Jesus when we talk about protection. His sinless blood was shed to pay the price for the guilty one. And because Jesus paid the price, we who are in Him have a right to walk in divine health and protection. Grace qualifies us for protection. When the devil accuses you, saying, "How dare you believe God for protection, when you are (he goes on to list your failures)," you just have to point to Jesus' blood, which has paid for all your failures. With grace as your basis, the God of peace can reign over your fears and impart to you unshakable faith for His protection.

3. The more you understand God's grace, the more you'll grow in your understanding of how perfectly your Father in heaven loves you. God *so* loved you and me, He sent His only begotten Son to die on the cross on our behalf, carrying all our sins upon His own body so that today, we can come boldly to His throne of grace. He did it so that today, we are not as sheep without a shepherd, but we are so deeply loved and cared for by our Abba Father. We are His children and when we call on Him, He WILL answer. We have a God who demonstrated His love for us *while* we were still sinners—when we had nothing to offer Him but our brokenness, our shame, our sins, and our disqualifications! Oh what perfect love!

4. "The Angel of the LORD" appeared to Gideon. In the Old Testament, this expression usually refers to our Lord Jesus in His preincarnate state. Jesus Himself appeared to Gideon when he was in the pit of fear and called him a "mighty man of valor" (Judg. 6:12).

5. When our Lord Jesus looks at you, He sees you as a *mighty man* *or mighty woman of courage.* It's not how we see ourselves that defines us; it is how our Lord Jesus sees us that defines us. That's why we read His Word to discover what He says about us. No matter what state you are in right now and how messed up your life might be, no matter how many times you have failed and even if people around you have given up on you, the Lord Jesus sees the best in you. He sees your potential, your gifting, your call, and your destiny to do great things in this life!

6. Talk to Jesus about upcoming decisions. He will lead and guide you with His peace. If there is peace from the Lord, then go with that decision. If there is an absence of peace and you feel a sense of restraint, then back away from it. You will find that guidance from the Lord comes very easily when God manifests Himself as *Jehovah Shalom*. In His peace, decisions don't feel forced and full of strife. In His peace, there is a rest.

7. Astoundingly, rather than rejecting Gideon, the Lord simply turned to him and said, "Go in this might of yours, and you shall save Israel from the hand of the Midianites. Have I not sent you?" (Judg. 6:14). I am so glad that the Lord is not like you and me. He always calls the things that are not as though they are (see Rom. 4:17). And I believe that as you receive a revelation of how the Lord is the God of peace in your life, you may be fearful and complaining now, but like Gideon, God will send you to be a testimony of His protection. He will send you to all your friends, coworkers, and loved ones who are bound by fear, and He will use you to deliver them from fear!

8. According to the *Strong's Concordance*, the word *shalom* refers to completeness, safety, soundness, welfare, health, and supply. It also refers to peace, quiet, tranquility, and contentment, as well as friendship in human relationships and with God in a covenant relationship.

9. As a child of God, you can claim His promise straightaway and say, "I will *not* be afraid of the disease that walks in darkness." Do the necessary medical checks and consult with medical professionals, but do it without fear. Lean on your *Jehovah Shalom*.

10. Because there is a realm that is higher than what we see in the natural, and I declare to you today that YOU SHALL NOT BE AFRAID. Fear is a spiritual condition, and cannot be combated with a natural answer, or by us trying to reason it away. The Bible tells us that the natural mind cannot understand things that are spiritual (see 1 Cor. 2:14). How can you not be afraid? By inviting the God of peace to reign in your life. As you do that, the robust peace of God, which surpasses all understanding, *will* guard your heart and mind through Christ Jesus (see Phil. 4:7).

11. "Peace I leave with you, My peace I give to you; not as the world gives do I give to you. Let not your heart be troubled, neither let it be afraid" (John 14:27).

CHAPTER 6

1. When negative thoughts come your way, do *not* give them time to take root. What begins in the mind can take root in your heart, and can even lead to adverse effects on your physical body. Counter those thoughts by quoting the written Word of God.

2. Three times our Lord Jesus was tempted by Satan in the wilderness. Each time, His response was the same—He quoted the *written* Word of God. Against each attack, His response was to say, "It is written" (see Matt. 4:1–11). In the first temptation, when the devil challenged our Lord Jesus to prove His identity, the Lord did not rely on what His Father had audibly spoken over Him at the River Jordan: "This is My beloved Son, in whom I am well pleased" (Matt. 3:17). Over and over again, our Lord declared, "It is written." Now, if the Son of God used "it is written" to defeat the devil, how much more you and I need to. When fear grips your heart or evil thoughts plague your mind, quote His written Word!

3. This is the time to declare, "It is written—'With long life I will satisfy him, and show him My salvation'" (Ps. 91:16) or "It is written—'Surely He shall deliver you from the snare of the fowler *and* from the perilous pestilence'" (Ps. 91:3).

5. That's when the Word's latent power becomes actual power. When our Lord Jesus was tempted in the wilderness, He did not merely think about Scripture. He spoke it out loud. You can memorize thousands of

Scriptures, but if you don't learn to say, "It is written," and release the Word, there will be no power. God's power is there, but it is all lying dormant inside you. The moment you speak it out, it is as if God is speaking. God's Word in *your* mouth is like God speaking. Amen!

6. "For God has not given us a spirit of fear, but of power and of love and of a sound mind" (2 Tim. 1:7).

7. If the fear comes back, speak the Word of God again! If the devil wants a fight, give him one! Give him the sword of the Spirit and he will get the *point* every time.

9. Megan took hold of 1 John 4:17—"as He is, so are we in this world"—believing that since Jesus does not have cancer, then neither does she!

10. On the pulpit at the front of his small church sanctuary was a plaque that he always looked at as a child when he got bored with the sermon he was hearing. He kept on reading those words until they entered his spirit and he believed them: "A thousand may fall at your side, and ten thousand at your right hand; *but* it shall not come near you."

CHAPTER 7

1. The Hebrew word for "trust" is *chacah*, which is the root word for "refuge" in Psalm 91. In other words, to make the Lord your refuge is to trust Him in all things. Trust Him with your plans, with your life, and with your family. Trust Him for His leading and wisdom. Confide in Him. Our Lord Jesus is not distant; He is not a Savior who is far away. He is so personal...so near you. There is safety and protection when we draw near to Him and dwell in His sweet presence, His Word, and His house.

2. At the cross, our Lord Jesus put all our sins, including the sin of crucifying Him, under the category of "unintentional" when He prayed, "Father, forgive them; for they know not what they do" (Luke 23:34 KJV). He was not just referring to Israel or the Romans; all *our* sins nailed Jesus to the cross. He chose the nails and offered us complete forgiveness. In it we see how good and merciful our God is!

3. Jesus is your city of refuge, and when you run to Him for refuge, the one seeking revenge (a picture of the devil) no longer has power over you. My friend, we were all sinners and the wages of sin is death (see Rom. 6:23). Before the cross, the devil had the legal right to put a death sentence over your head because of your sins. But the good news of the gospel is that Jesus took that death sentence at the cross, and in Christ we can receive His forgiveness and His protection. Hallelujah!

4. The message is: You can find sanctuary (Kedesh) on the Lord's strong shoulders (Shechem), which He offers in fellowship (Hebron). He is our fortress (Bezer) and He highly exalts (Ramoth) us above all our troubles with great rejoicing (Golan).

The names paint a stunning picture of our Lord Jesus, stooping down to where we are, and offering His stronger shoulders to us when we are fearful and weary. What a beautiful picture of the Good Shepherd rescuing His lost sheep! When we have failed and are completely worn out by the fights of life, He offers His shoulders in fellowship. He is our sanctuary. He is our safe refuge, where we are set apart from the world.

5. God invites us to consent to be protected. He wants us to be on His shoulders, in the safety of Himself as our impenetrable fortress. In this place, no predator can attack His sheep. On His shoulders, you are highly exalted above all your troubles, above all danger, all attacks, and far above all principalities and powers. Yes, far above Satan, above all the powers of darkness and the snare of the fowler. On His shoulders, you are far above every sickness, disease, and every name that is named. What a great place to be!

6. Deuteronomy 33:12 tells us, "The beloved of the LORD shall dwell in safety by Him, *who* shelters him all the day long; and he shall dwell between His shoulders." The safest place you can be today is on His shoulders. Jesus is your city of refuge. In your day of trouble, run to Him!

7. The church is not man's idea; it is God's idea. It is a place where all the guilty, where all who are suffering from condemnation, and where those who are being pursued can come and take refuge. You see, it is not God's heart for you to take this journey of faith on your own. Certainly, you can learn a lot by reading books or watching sermons online, but God's heart is for you to be part of a *community* of faith.

8. The apostle Paul declares, "And He put all *things* under His feet, and gave Him *to be* head over all *things* to the church, which is His body, the fullness of Him who fills all in all" (Eph. 1:22–23). Today, in our broken and fallen world, this power and dominion is found in the church! His power, His authority, and His fullness are all found in the church—our city of refuge where we can run to and find divine protection!

10. When the mini cyclone hit her street, Iris declared, "Thank You, Jesus, that You are the calm in the storm!" Many surrounding houses, cars, and trees were damaged, but when the cyclone came near her house, it stopped completely and turned around, leaving her house, family car, and backyard tree undamaged!

CHAPTER 8

1. Without faltering, Elisha calmly told his servant, "Do not fear, for those who *are* with us *are* more than those who *are* with them" (2 Kings 6:16).

2. He saw that the hillside around them was filled with blindingly magnificent horses and chariots of fire. God's army of angels. They were all around them, flanking them on every side, ablaze with the glory of the Most High. Their beauty and majesty were beyond what the servant could imagine, and as he marveled, he realized that the Syrian forces, which had looked so formidable just moments ago, were now utterly dwarfed by the angelic army.

3. The two men saw different things. The young man saw the great Syrian army. But Elisha saw an *even greater* angelic army on chariots of fire.

4. Whether you find yourself besieged by debts, attacked by what doctors call a terminal illness, or constantly anxious over the safety of your children, remember this verse: "Do not fear, for those who *are* with us *are* more than those who *are* with them" (2 Kings 6:16). The God of angelic armies is with you. No weapon formed against you shall prosper (see Isa. 54:17)!

5. Let me illustrate it like this: If I were a general in the army and I said to a captain, "Captain, I give you charge over Private Ryan," it means that this captain must protect Private Ryan at all costs, because Private Ryan is now under his charge. Do you see? In the same way the angels surrounded Elisha and his servant and protected them, they are surrounding us and protecting us today *because God has given them charge over us to protect us!*

6. The devil didn't want to say those words, "to keep you in all your ways," because that would be tantamount to reminding believers of Proverbs 3:6–7—to acknowledge God in all our ways. So he conveniently left out that whole portion. But praise the Lord, we know that *this* is what the Lord has promised: "For He shall give His angels charge over you, **to keep you in all your ways**" (boldface mine). Our part is to simply acknowledge Him in all our ways, and He shall direct our paths, protecting us along the way!

7. It is saying that as you go about your daily walk, the Lord will protect you. The Hebrew word for "ways" in verse 11 shows this clearly—it is the word *derek*, which means path, road, or journey. As you go about your daily path, whether going to work or heading home, there are times when the enemy may have put snares ahead of you that you are unaware of. But God will give His angels charge over you, to go ahead of you to protect you from those snares.

8. What Mark 16:18 is saying is that should you drink something harmful without realizing it in the course of your day, the Lord will protect you from being harmed! However, if someone challenges you to drink poison and you willfully drink it to show that it will not hurt you, that's just being foolish. Psalm 91:11 is talking about the paths you take as part of your normal life. Drinking poison intentionally is certainly not part of your normal life.

9. The Lord has given His angels charge over us. The New Living Translation says that the Lord will "order his angels to protect you wherever you go." The Amplified version says that His angels will "**accompany** *and* **defend** *and* **preserve** you in all your ways" (boldface mine). This gives us such assurance that we are covered under His wings of refuge and protection!

10. Because He had already chosen to go to the cross and to die the death that we deserved. He gave up His protection so that today, you and I can claim all the promises of His protection. And as joint heirs with Christ (see Rom. 8:17), each one of us can summon twelve legions of angels!

11. The most important key is *worship*. As you offer your praise to the Lord, that's when angels are most active. Psalm 34:7 tells us that "The angel of the LORD encamps all around those who **fear** Him, and delivers them" (boldface mine). Our Lord Jesus defined "fear" as "worship" for us. When Satan tempted Him in the wilderness, He responded by quoting a verse in Deuteronomy that says, "You shall fear the LORD your God" (Deut. 6:13). But He changed the word "fear" to "worship" and said to the devil, "For it is written, 'You shall **worship** the LORD your God'" (Matt. 4:10, boldface mine).

13. Every time you quote Scriptures out loud, you are giving voice to His Word, and angels will respond. When you say, "Father, I thank You that no evil shall befall me today, nor shall any plague or disease come near my dwelling," angels harken to the voice of the Word of God being spoken. Angels cannot read your mind—so speak forth His Word!

CHAPTER 9

1. In Christ, we have authority over the devil and all his cohorts. In Christ, we have authority to *tread upon the lion and the cobra*. The fowler's snares shall be foiled and the hunter shall be the hunted. Our role in this increasingly dangerous world isn't to be passive and indifferent. We're not called to be sitting ducks, waiting to be devoured by the roaring lion. We are endued with power and authority to hunt down the roaring lion!

2. When Samson was accosted by the lion, "the Spirit of the LORD came mightily upon him, and he tore the lion apart as one would have torn apart a young goat, though *he had* nothing in his hand" (Judg. 14:6). Now, *that's* taking authority! The hunter came at Samson but found itself the hunted!

3. From this strong predator that had come against him, Samson received something sweet. The spiritual truth for us is that out of every evil and negative thing the devil throws at you today, God will make something sweet for you. Your giants will be as bread to you. God will turn every bitter adversity into sweet honey for you!

4. She and her husband prayed, speaking God's Word over his body, *and* she commanded the negative symptoms to go in Jesus' name, as the apostle Peter did in the book of Acts (see Acts 3:6).

5. We are praying according to the Word of God and wielding the sword of the Spirit. So no matter what report is roaring at you, be it from doctors, bankers, or from the news media, take your place of authority and lay hold of Scriptures for your situation. Fight back with the Word of God!

6. Proverbs 19:12 says, "The king's wrath *is* like **the roaring of a lion**" (boldface mine). The devil is a liar and an imposter. He goes about as a roaring lion because he is imitating the King of kings, our Lord Jesus, the real lion of Judah. He wants people to think that our King is full of wrath, anger, and rage against us. He comes at us roaring with the voice of condemnation, accusation, and shame.

7. Because if you believe that about God, you won't take refuge under the shelter of His wings or your rightful place of authority, power, and strength. You will feel unworthy of God's promises and won't pray the prayer of protection. When you run away from God, you are running straight into the devil's snare. You abdicate your place of authority when you abdicate your place of intimacy with God.

8. You are loved. God is not mad at you. In Christ, you can have the confident assurance that you are forgiven, loved, and righteous (see Eph. 1:7, Rom. 8:37, 2 Cor. 5:21). The Lord Jesus has taken all your punishment at the cross so that today, you can enjoy His undeserved, unearned, and unmerited favor. Because God sees you *in Christ*, who is completely spotless and without blame, you can come boldly to His throne of grace (see Heb. 4:16) and dwell in the secret place with the King of kings, where the phony "roaring lion" has no power over you!

9. God's wrath against our sins was completely satisfied at Calvary, and today we are beneficiaries of His favor. In Hebrew, the word used for "favor" is *ratsown*, which means His pleasure, delight, goodwill, and acceptance. Our place of protection was purchased with the blood of our Lord Jesus Christ. In Him, we have been made righteous, and all the blessings of the righteous, including protection, provision, and length of days, are our inheritance.

10. This persecution involves other people who come against you when you live a godly life and preach the gospel of Jesus Christ. Be clear that it doesn't involve terminal illnesses, tragic accidents, or premature death.

11. One of Job's complaints was this: "If only there were a mediator between us, someone who could bring us together" (Job 9:33 NLT). The powerful words spoken by Elihu in Job 33:23–25 describe this mediator and foreshadow what our Lord Jesus Christ would do and be for us. First Timothy 2:5–6 tells us, "For *there is* one God and one Mediator between God and men, the Man Christ Jesus, who gave Himself a ransom for all, to be testified in due time." Job experienced his sufferings because he didn't have a mediator, but today, we do—in the person of our Lord Jesus.

12. The atoning blood of Christ has canceled all the legal rights that the enemy had against you and your family. When we receive all that His perfect sacrifice at the cross has accomplished for us, we will see Him deliver us from the pit. Today, you don't have to live afraid that you will be like Job. Unlike Job, you have a mediator—Christ Jesus. In Him you can look forward to a future full of His promises, blessings, and protection (see Ps. 23:6)!

13. Philippians 1:21–25 describes Paul as torn between departing and being with Christ and remaining and continuing to do fruitful work for Christ. Acts 14:19–21 records Paul being stoned and left for dead, but death had no hold on him—he got up and continued preaching. In Acts 28:3–6, Paul was bitten by a poisonous snake but was completely unharmed. But in 2 Timothy 4:6–8 (his last epistle), Paul had decided that he had fought a good fight and had finished the race. It was enough; he was satisfied. We see here a man with authority over death. Paul was not murdered; he was ready to go.

14. Psalm 91:16 says, "With long life I will **satisfy you**." This tells us that all of us have a free choice to use our faith to believe God for a long life. How long a life? That depends on you—according to your faith and satisfaction be it unto you. The same authority over the enemy that the apostle Paul had belongs to you and me today.

CHAPTER 10

1. God SO loved the world that He sent His only begotten Son to save and ransom us. The Lord Jesus Christ Himself fulfilled *all* the requirements of the law. Today, even when our love for Him wavers, even when we fail, He still delivers us from evil! First John 4:10 encapsulates the crux of the new covenant of grace: "In this is love, **not that we loved God, but that He loved us** and sent His Son *to be* the propitiation [the atoning sacrifice] for our sins" (boldface mine). The emphasis of the new covenant is God's love for you, not your love for God. Our love for Him will always waver, but "the steadfast love of the Lord **never ceases**; his mercies never come to an end" (Lam. 3:22–23 ESV, boldface mine).

2. We can receive the promise of Psalm 5:12, which declares, "For You, O Lord, will bless the righteous; with favor You will surround him as *with* a shield." Naturally, we can't always watch our backs. But supernaturally, God has got us covered all around. His abundant supply of grace (unmerited favor) encompasses us like a mighty and impenetrable force field, surrounding us 360 degrees and twenty-four hours a day!

3. We set our love upon God by meditating on, talking about, and listening to preaching about His love for us! Remember, it is not about our love for Him, but His love for us. It is about us meditating on Bible verses such as John 3:16. There is protection and deliverance from destruction when you believe in God's love for you. Set your mind on how greatly loved and dearly prized you are. The more conscious you are of the Lord's love for you, the more His protection will manifest in your life!

4. Daniel was clearly a man who dwelt daily in the secret place of the Most High, under the shadow of His wings. Daniel set his heart toward the Lord, praying and giving thanks to God three times a day. We also see one of God's angels in action and Daniel taking authority over fearsome, hungry lions. In fact, he did not even suffer a single scratch after being shut up in a den full of lions for a whole night. Truly, the Lord was Daniel's refuge and fortress.

5. Daniel's dedicated prayer time was an outward expression of the *closeness and intimacy* he had with the Lord. There are no formulas, steps, or shortcuts to walking in divine protection. Simply walk close with the Lord and you will unconsciously be under the shadow of His wings. Don't just pursue the protection, seek the Protector! You can recite Psalm 91 fifty times a day, but if you have no relationship with Jesus, there will be no results. The prayer of protection is not transactional; it is *relational*.

It is so good to live with thanksgiving in your heart toward the Lord. Each and every day, there are so many things that our Lord protects us from that we are not even aware of. Give thanks to Him for His love for you. Praise Him and set your mind daily toward Him. Be so conscious of how close you are to Him and how utterly loved you are— and enjoy the protection that comes from being found in the shadow of His wings!

6. Because our Lord Jesus has been punished on the cross in your place, the devil cannot come to the King and demand that you be punished. Your sins were forgiven not because the King simply decided to close an eye and let you off the hook. The King forgave your sins *righteously* after judging them in the body of our Lord Jesus Christ. He who was completely without sin took your place and bore the full weight of the punishment for your sins (see 2 Cor. 5:21). ALL your sins have been legally and judicially judged at the cross. Because of His finished work, once you received the Lord Jesus into your heart, God's justice and righteousness are on your side!

7. None of us would ever fully comprehend what God experienced in sending His own beloved Son to the cross. We catch just a small glimpse of the torment that God suffered when we read about King Darius's suffering. King Darius wanted to save Daniel, but he could not violate his own law. Similarly, God loves His Son, but He knew the only way to save us, who had violated the law, was to sacrifice His own Son, Jesus Christ.

8. Our Lord Jesus came to reveal the name "Father." *Father* speaks of family and of closeness and intimacy. You can know God as *Elyon*, the Most High. As *El Shaddai*, God Almighty. As *Yehovah*, the Lord, the covenant-keeping God. As *Elohim*, mighty Creator of the heavens and the earth. Every name is so significant as each one reveals a wonderful aspect of our God. But when you know God as *Father*, *all* His virtues, attributes, and power work *for* you to set you on high and deliver you.

9. Jesus prayed, "Holy Father, keep through Your name those whom You have given Me, that they may be one as We *are*" (John 17:11). The Greek word for "keep" here is the word *tereo*, which means to attend to carefully, to take care of, to guard, to watch, and to preserve. And the name through which you will be kept guarded and protected is FATHER. Beloved, I want you to know beyond the shadow of a doubt that you have a heavenly Father who loves you, who gave up His all for you, and who is vigilantly watching over you!

10. Goshen means "drawing near." He wanted them in a place of nearness to him and he told them, "There **I will provide** for you" (Gen. 45:10–11, boldface mine). Beloved, even in the midst of famine, Jesus, our heavenly Joseph, wants us close to Him so He can provide for us.

11. First, God "set apart the land of Goshen" (Exod. 8:22), where His people dwelt. In that place, they were protected from all the ten plagues that besieged the land of Egypt. Second, in the second last of the ten plagues, a thick, paralyzing darkness covered the land of Egypt for three whole days. Yet, during that time, "all the children of Israel had light in their dwellings" (Exod. 10:23). It was a supernatural darkness that covered Egypt, and it was a supernatural light that the Israelites enjoyed in Goshen, a light the darkness tried to smother but couldn't.

12. Even when there's thick and deep darkness all around, the church—you and I, together with our families—can experience and enjoy God's supernatural light in our dwellings. We, who have been drawn near to Him through the work of His Son, can have intimacy with God and enjoy His protective covering to live fear-free and victoriously in these dark times.

CHAPTER 11

1. Because of the divine exchange that took place at the cross, where our Lord Jesus cried out, "My God, My God, why have You forsaken Me?" (Matt. 27:46). He was forsaken—left helpless, totally abandoned, and deserted—so that today, we can have the confidence that our heavenly Father will never leave us nor forsake us (see Heb. 13:5). What a Savior!

2. Our part is to simply *call upon* our Savior, Jesus Christ! He wants you to cast "**all** your care upon Him, for **He cares for you**" (1 Pet. 5:7, boldface mine). Whatever you are troubled or anxious about, call upon Him and allow His peace to supernaturally guard your heart in every area that you are troubled. The Bible says, "Be anxious for nothing, but in everything by prayer and supplication, with thanksgiving, let your requests be made known to God; and the peace of God, which surpasses all understanding, will guard your hearts and minds through Christ Jesus" (Phil. 4:6–7).

3. She called out the name of Jesus at least five times. No matter what situation we are in, the Lord is with us and will surely deliver us when we call upon His name!

4. They said, "O Nebuchadnezzar, we do not need to defend ourselves before you. If we are thrown into the blazing furnace, the God whom we serve is able to save us. He will rescue us from your power, Your Majesty. But even if he doesn't…we will never serve your gods or worship the gold statue you have set up" (Dan. 3:16–18 NLT).

5. As King Nebuchadnezzar acknowledged, God honored the three young men and "sent His Angel and delivered His servants who trusted in Him" (Dan. 3:28). One "like the Son of God" walked with them in the midst of the fire (Dan. 3:25). The fire did not touch them, not a hair of their heads was singed, and their clothing was not scorched. In fact, the flames only served to loose them from their bonds. Not only did God receive great glory through the king's proclamation, but the king also promoted the three men to even higher positions in the province of Babylon.

6. As you call upon the Lord in your day of trouble, the trial you are going through will have no power over you; it will not even leave a smell on you. Instead, the only smell on you will be the fragrance of the Lord Jesus (see 2 Cor. 2:14)! As the people around you witness how the Lord delivers you, may they come to know His wonderful name and give Him praise. Instead of being negatively affected by the trials you face, you will receive honor and promotion just like Shadrach, Meshach, and Abednego.

8. First Corinthians 1:30 tells us that Christ has become for us wisdom from God. So what we really need is the Lord Jesus. We need to lean on Him and draw close to Him daily. He is our wisdom and only He can cause us to always be at the right place at the right time. Many troubles and dangerous situations can be completely avoided when we don't depend on our own wisdom and planning, but involve the Lord in all that we do (see Prov. 3:6).

10. First ask the Lord for His wisdom and leading. Isaiah 11:2–3 NASB says of the Lord that "the spirit of wisdom and understanding" will rest on Him, and "He will not judge by what His eyes see, nor make a decision by what His ears hear." There is a discernment and wisdom from the Lord that goes beyond looking at the outward appearance of a matter. When you call on Him, He will answer you and give you an answer of peace. If you don't feel a peace to proceed, don't allow anyone to pressure you into making a decision you will regret!

11. Closed doors are not necessarily negative, and could be signs of God's protection over our lives. As we plan and schedule our busy lives, we need to make room for the Lord to intervene and to guide us to be at the right place at the right time. Proverbs 16:9 says, "A man's heart plans his way, but the Lord directs his steps." Even as we plan, we must always remember to commit all our ways to the Lord, and allow *Him* to direct our steps.

12. No, when you walk close to the Lord and have a close relationship with Him, He can lead you in supernaturally natural ways. The testimony of the couple whose lives were spared from the tsunami reflects this. They had moved locations because the wife felt like eating something in another location some distance away from the beachfront. We need the Lord to direct *all* our steps!

CHAPTER 12

1. Long life is not just in terms of *quantity*—the number of days—but also *quality*—health and strength. Caleb lived long and remained strong. The Bible says Caleb was as strong at eighty-five as he was when he was forty-five. Which means in the last forty years in the harsh wilderness, his strength, youth, and vigor didn't diminish. There was no leaking, no receding, and no fading away of his strength!

2. At eighty-five, Caleb was not ready to pack it up and slow down. He was ready to pick a fight with *giants* and to take great and fortified cities to gain possession of a mountain! This was not just some trash-talking babble; Caleb did as he said (see Josh. 14:13–14)!

3. Joshua 14:14 records that "Hebron therefore became the inheritance of Caleb...because he **wholly followed** the LORD God of Israel" (boldface mine). His secret to long life was found in simply *following* the Lord. "Hebron" was the name for one of the cities of refuge we talked about in chapter 7. In Hebrew, "Hebron" means fellowship or association. This speaks of intimacy, closeness, and connection with the Lord, which is what the prayer of protection is all about.

4. Our Lord Jesus is the way, the truth, and the life (see John 14:6). He came that we might have life and have it more abundantly (see John 10:10). *Follow* Him and find the path to a long and abundant life. Everything Caleb experienced was under the old covenant. His renewal of youth and unabated strength and vigor were all experienced under the old covenant. *How much more* should we be experiencing this renewal of youth, boundless energy, and length of days under the new covenant of grace that is established on better promises (see Heb. 8:6)!

5. It is important that we interpret this psalm in the context of the children of Israel being in the wilderness and under God's wrath. We have also seen that even under the old covenant, Caleb transcended this life span and was still going strong at eighty-five years old.

6. God has promised, "With long life I will **satisfy him**, and show him My salvation" (Ps. 91:16, boldface mine). *Your satisfaction* is the limit and according to your faith, be it unto you. As you stay close to our Lord Jesus, you will live long, live strong, and live under the protective covering of His wings.

7. The Hebrew word for "salvation" is *yeshua*. And *Yeshua* is the Hebrew name of our Lord Jesus! This is what God was saying: "With long life I will satisfy him, and show him My *Yeshua*." Long life is found in our *Yeshua*. You can know God as *El Elyon*, God Most High, as the Almighty *Shaddai*, as *Jehovah*, and even as *Elohim*, but the name that gives you full and utter confidence is the name Jesus!

8. *Jesus died young that we may live long.* And not just live long in this world. At the cross, He purchased for us the gift of eternal life, paid for with His own blood. The moment you received Jesus as your Lord and Savior, your salvation in Him was sure and secure!

9. Second Timothy 4:18 declares, "And the Lord will deliver me from **every evil work** and preserve *me* for His heavenly kingdom" (boldface mine).

10. Jesus defined it as the *worship* of the Lord. In the wilderness temptation (see Matt. 4:8–10), our Lord said, "You shall worship the LORD your God, and Him only you shall serve." He was quoting from Deuteronomy 6:13, which says, "You shall fear the LORD your God and serve Him." Our Lord substituted the word "fear" with the word "worship."

12. In contrast to the tabernacle of Moses, the tabernacle of David had no veil separating man and God. David and the priests could go directly to worship the Lord before the ark of the covenant.

13. God is saying that the way into the Holy of Holies is open! Through Christ, there is no longer any separation between God and man. *Whosoever* believes in Jesus shall never perish. Hallelujah!

WE WOULD LIKE TO HEAR FROM YOU

If you have a testimony to share after reading this book, please send it to us via JosephPrince.com/testimony.

STAY CONNECTED WITH JOSEPH

Connect with Joseph through these social media channels and receive daily inspirational teachings:

Facebook.com/JosephPrince
Twitter.com/JosephPrince
Youtube.com/JosephPrinceOnline
Instagram: @JosephPrince

FREE DAILY E-MAIL DEVOTIONAL

Sign up for Joseph's FREE daily e-mail devotional at JosephPrince.com/meditate and receive bite-size inspirations to help you grow in grace.

BOOKS BY JOSEPH PRINCE

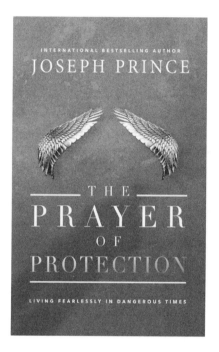

The Prayer of Protection

We live in dangerous times. A time in which terrorist activities, pandemics, and natural calamities are on the rise. But there is good news. God has given us a powerful prayer of protection—Psalm 91—through which we and our families can find safety and deliverance from every snare of the enemy. In *The Prayer of Protection*, discover a God of love and His impenetrable shield of protection that covers everything that concerns you, and start living fearlessly in these dangerous times!

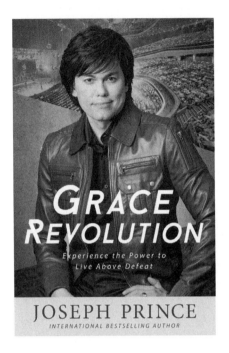

Grace Revolution

Experience the revolution that is sweeping across the world! In *Grace Revolution*, Joseph Prince offers five powerful keys that will help you experience firsthand the grace revolution in your own life, and live above defeat. See how these keys can work easily for you, as you read inspiring stories of people who experienced amazing and lasting transformations when they encountered the real Jesus and heard the unadulterated gospel. Whatever your challenge today, begin to step away from defeat and take a massive leap toward your victory. Get your copy today and let the revolution begin in your life!

The Power of Right Believing

Experience transformation, breakthroughs, and freedom today through the power of right believing! This book offers seven practical and powerful keys that will help you find freedom from all fears, guilt, and addictions. See these keys come alive in the many precious testimonies you will read from people around the world who have experienced breakthroughs and liberty from all kinds of bondages. Win the battle for your mind through understanding the powerful truths of God's Word and begin a journey of victorious living and unshakable confidence in God's love for you!

Destined to Reign

This pivotal and quintessential book on the grace of God will change your life forever! Join Joseph Prince as he unlocks foundational truths to understanding God's grace and how it alone sets you free to experience victory over every adversity, lack, and destructive habit that is limiting you today. Be uplifted and refreshed as you discover how reigning in life is all about Jesus and what He has already done for you. Start experiencing the success, wholeness, and victory that you were destined to enjoy!

Unmerited Favor

This follow-up book to *Destined To Reign* is a must-read if you want to live out the dreams that God has birthed in your heart! Building on the foundational truths of God's grace laid out in *Destined To Reign*, *Unmerited Favor* takes you into a deeper understanding of the gift of righteousness that you have through the cross and how it gives you a supernatural ability to succeed in life. Packed with empowering new covenant truths, *Unmerited Favor* will set you free to soar above your challenges and lead an overcoming life as God's beloved today.

ABOUT THE AUTHOR

JOSEPH PRINCE is a leading voice in proclaiming the gospel of grace to a whole new generation of believers and leaders. He is the senior pastor of New Creation Church in Singapore, a vibrant and dynamic church with a congregation of more than 30,000 attendees. He separately heads Joseph Prince Ministries, one of the fastest-growing television broadcast ministries in the world today, reaching millions with the gospel of grace. Joseph is also the bestselling author of *The Power of Right Believing* and *Destined To Reign*, and a highly sought-after conference speaker. For more information about his other inspiring resources, visit www.JosephPrince.com.